MICHEL ROUX

Desserts

Photography by SIMON WHEELER

THE MASTER CHEFS

WEIDENFELD & NICOLSON

LONDON

MICHEL ROUX's delicious desserts have made him famous throughout the world. He began his career as a pastry chef apprentice at the Pâtisserie Loyal in Paris, and then worked for the British Embassy in Paris and for Mlle Cecile de Rothschild.

With his brother Albert, he opened Le Gavroche in London in 1967. The Waterside Inn at Bray in Berkshire opened in 1972 and since then has consistently won many major international gastronomy awards.

Michel Roux was awarded Meilleur Ouvrier de France en Pâtisserie in 1976 and received the Chevalier de l'Ordre National du Mérite in 1986 and the Chevalier de l'Ordre des Arts et des Lettres in 1990.

With Albert, he has written several books, including *New Classic Cuisine* (1983), *Roux Brothers on Pâtisserie* (1986), *At Home with the Roux Brothers* (1988), which accompanied a BBC television series, *French Country Cooking* (1989) and *Cooking for Two* (1991). He published *Desserts – A Lifelong Passion* in 1994.

CONTENTS

BLACKBERRY CLAFOUTIS 8

PEAR AND GINGER SABAYON 10

BANANA RAMEKINS
with caramel topping 12

RASPBERRY ICE CREAM 14

WARM PEACH FEUILLETÉS 16

CHOCOLATE CRÈME BRÛLÉE 18

SURPRISE ORANGE PANCAKES 20

TUTTI FRUTTI CHOUX PUFFS   22

HOT GRAND MARNIER SOUFFLÉS
with orange segments   24

APPLE HEDGEHOG   26

THE BASICS   28
    QUICK PUFF PASTRY
    PASTRY CREAM
    CHOUX PASTE

The dessert, being the last course of the meal, must always be the most exciting part, and therefore needs to be light and delicate to encourage the palate to be tempted further.

INTRODUCTION

Maybe I am biased, because I began my career as a pastry chef, but I consider dessert to be one of the most important parts of a meal, like the final act of a play. It need not be a complicated assembly of different elements: a refined dessert may be simple and elegant, and a well-made old favourite will always be welcome.

I have chosen these ten desserts to be both varied and visually appealing: pear and ginger sabayon a mountain of pale foam; chocolate crème brûlée with a deep golden surface, hard and shiny as a mirror; creamy apple mousse spiked with apple crisps to resemble a hedgehog. A soufflé is an exciting way to end a meal, and really not difficult – try it once or twice and you will soon gain confidence. Of course, a soufflé must be cooked just before serving, but there are plenty of ideas for desserts that can be made in advance: pure-tasting raspberry ice cream; blackberry clafoutis, a variation on a French country classic; and choux puffs, light as a cloud and filled with fresh summer berries.

BLACKBERRY CLAFOUTIS

250 G/9 OZ QUICK PUFF PASTRY
   (PAGE 28)
4 EGGS
200 G/7 OZ CASTER SUGAR
25 G/1 OZ FLOUR
125 ML/4 FL OZ MILK
125 ML/4 FL OZ DOUBLE CREAM
2 TABLESPOONS KIRSCH (OPTIONAL)
250 G/9 OZ BLACKBERRIES
2 TABLESPOONS GRANULATED
   SUGAR

SERVES 8

On a lightly floured work surface, roll out the pastry to form a circle, 2 mm/¹⁄₁₆ inch thick. Use to line a greased, loose-bottomed 24 cm/ 9½ inch diameter tart tin and cut off any excess pastry around the rim. Chill for 20 minutes.

Preheat the oven to 220°C/ 425°F/Gas Mark 7. Prick the pastry with a fork, line it with greaseproof paper and fill with baking beans. Bake blind for 20 minutes, then remove from the oven; remove the beans and paper. Reduce the oven temperature to 200°C/400°F/Gas Mark 6.

Put the eggs and caster sugar in a bowl, whisk together for 2 minutes, then add the flour and whisk for a further 2 minutes. Still whisking, add the milk, cream and kirsch, if using. Spread the blackberries over the pastry, pour in the cream mixture and bake for 30 minutes or until just set. As soon as the clafoutis is cooked, remove the outside of the tart tin, leaving the clafoutis on the base.

Just before serving, sprinkle the granulated sugar over the barely warm clafoutis.

PEAR AND GINGER SABAYON

4 EGG YOLKS

50 G/2 OZ CASTER SUGAR

3 TABLESPOONS COLD WATER

100 ML/3½ FL OZ PEAR EAU-DE-VIE

50 G/2 OZ PRESERVED GINGER IN
   SYRUP, DRAINED AND
   FINELY CHOPPED

SERVES 6

First prepare a bain-marie: half-fill with cold water a saucepan large enough to hold the base of a mixing bowl.

Place all the ingredients in the mixing bowl and start whisking with a balloon whisk. Set the base of the bowl in the bain-marie and place over medium heat. Whisk continuously for 10–12 minutes; the temperature of the water in the bain-marie should not exceed 90°C/195°F or the sabayon will start to coagulate. If necessary, turn off or reduce the heat under the pan. Keep whisking until the sabayon becomes glossy and has the consistency of half-risen egg whites. The texture should be unctuous, frothy and light (the temperature should not exceed 55°C/130°F). As soon as the sabayon is ready, stop whisking, spoon it into bowls or large glasses and serve immediately.

BANANA RAMEKINS
with caramel topping

5–6 BANANAS, NOT TOO RIPE
JUICE OF 2 LEMONS
150 G/5 OZ BUTTER
150 G/5 OZ CASTER SUGAR
600 G/1¼ LB PASTRY CREAM
  (PAGE 29)
150 ML/¼ PINT DOUBLE CREAM
6 TABLESPOONS DARK RUM

SERVES 4–8 (1 OR 2 RAMEKINS EACH)

Peel the bananas, cut them into 1 cm/½ inch rounds and mix them with the lemon juice in a bowl.

Heat the butter in a frying pan, sprinkle on 85 g/3 oz of the caster sugar, add the banana rounds and lightly brown them over high heat for 2 minutes. Transfer to a plate and set aside.

In a bowl, whisk together the pastry cream, double cream and rum. Place a spoonful of this cream into each of eight small ramekins, about 9 cm/3½ inches in diameter.

Reserve the eight best banana rounds for decoration, then divide the rest between the ramekins. Fill up the ramekins with the cream, smooth the surface with a palette knife and sprinkle the tops with the remaining caster sugar. Caramelize the sugar with a blowtorch or under a very hot salamander or grill. Place two ramekins on each plate and garnish each ramekin with a reserved banana round. Serve at once.

RASPBERRY ICE CREAM

400 G/14 OZ FRESH OR FROZEN
RASPBERRIES
100 ML/3½ FL OZ COLD WATER
200 G/7 OZ CASTER SUGAR
JUICE OF 2 LEMONS
3 TABLESPOONS RASPBERRY EAU-
DE-VIE OR KIRSCH (OPTIONAL)
300 ML/½ PINT DOUBLE CREAM,
WHIPPED TO A RIBBON
CONSISTENCY

SERVES 6

Purée the raspberries with the water in a liquidizer for 2 minutes. Pass the purée through a wire-mesh conical sieve into a large bowl, rubbing and pushing it through with the back of a ladle.

Add the sugar to the resulting raspberry juice, then add the lemon juice and eau-de-vie or kirsch, if using, and whisk together. Fold in the cream, transfer the mixture to an ice-cream maker and churn for about 15 minutes or until the ice cream is velvety and half-frozen. Transfer to a bowl and freeze, or serve immediately.

Blackberries can be substituted for the raspberries.

WARM PEACH FEUILLETÉS

350 G/13 OZ QUICK PUFF PASTRY
    (PAGE 28)
150 G/5 OZ GRANULATED SUGAR
500 ML/16 FL OZ WATER
4 VERY RIPE PEACHES, SKINNED
EGGWASH (1 EGG WHITE MIXED
    WITH 1 TABLESPOON MILK)
40 G/1½ OZ ICING SUGAR
1 TABLESPOON GRENADINE SYRUP

SERVES 4
On a lightly floured work surface,
roll out the pastry to about 5 mm/
¼ inch thick. Using a 9 cm/
3½ inch pastry cutter, cut out four
circles and place them on a baking
sheet lightly moistened with cold
water. Chill for 20 minutes.

Place the granulated sugar and
the water in a saucepan and bring
to the boil over low heat, stirring
occasionally until the sugar has
dissolved. Add the peaches and
poach until just tender. Using a
slotted spoon, lift the peaches out
of the syrup; reserve the syrup.

Preheat the oven to 220°C/
425°F/Gas Mark 7. Brush the tops
of the pastry circles with eggwash.
Lightly press a 7 cm/2¾ inch pastry
cutter on to the circles to mark out

the lids. With the tip of a knife,
score criss-crosses on the lids.

Bake the pastry circles in the
oven for 10 minutes, then sprinkle
them with the icing sugar and bake
for another 2–3 minutes, until the
sugar forms an attractive glaze.

Slide the pastry circles on to a
wire rack. Run the tip of a knife
around the marked lids and detach
them carefully, lifting them off
with the knife.

Put 85 ml/3 fl oz of the
poaching syrup and the grenadine
in a small saucepan and simmer
over low heat until reduced by half.

Place a peach in each pastry
case and put them on individual
plates. Lightly coat the peaches
with the reduced syrup and
arrange the lids aslant at the edge
of the pastry cases. Serve at once.

CHOCOLATE CRÈME BRÛLÉE

300 G/11 OZ BITTER COUVERTURE
    OR BEST-QUALITY PLAIN DARK
    CHOCOLATE (ABOUT 64%
    COCOA SOLIDS)
500 ML/16 FL OZ MILK
500 ML/16 FL OZ DOUBLE CREAM
3 TABLESPOONS LIQUID GLUCOSE
8 EGG YOLKS
150 G/5 OZ CASTER SUGAR

SERVES 8

Break the chocolate into a large bowl and sit the bowl over a saucepan half-filled with hot water. Leave to melt, stirring occasionally until smooth.

Place the milk, cream and liquid glucose in a saucepan and bring to the boil over low heat, whisking occasionally.

In a bowl, whisk the egg yolks with 50 g/2 oz of the sugar until just pale.

Whisking continuously, pour the boiling milk mixture on to the melted chocolate. When it is thoroughly combined, pour the mixture on to the egg yolk mixture, whisking all the time.

Preheat the oven to 90°C/ 195°F/Gas Mark ¼. Divide the chocolate cream mixture between eight gratin dishes, about 15 cm/ 6 inches in diameter, and cook for 40 minutes or until just set.

Slide the dishes on to a wire rack and leave to cool at room temperature. Place in the refrigerator for a very short time.

Just before serving, sprinkle 2 teaspoons caster sugar evenly over each crème brûlée and caramelize with a blowtorch or under a very hot salamander or grill. Place each one on a plate and serve at once.

The contrast between the warm, crunchy topping and the lightly chilled cream is delicious. To reach the cream you will need to tap the top sharply with a spoon to crack it open, as shown in the picture.

SURPRISE ORANGE PANCAKES

150 G/5 OZ FLOUR

25 G/1 OZ CASTER SUGAR

PINCH OF SALT

2 EGGS

300 ML/½ PINT MILK

6 TABLESPOONS DOUBLE CREAM

CLARIFIED BUTTER FOR COOKING
    THE PANCAKES

400 G/14 OZ PASTRY CREAM
    (PAGE 29)

GRATED ZEST AND JUICE OF
    2 ORANGES, JUICE SIMMERED
    UNTIL REDUCED BY HALF

40 G/1½ OZ ICING SUGAR

SERVES 6

Sift the flour into a bowl and mix in the caster sugar and salt. Lightly whisk in the eggs, then the milk, a little at a time. When the mixture is thoroughly combined, stir in the cream, cover with clingfilm and leave the batter to rest for at least 1 hour.

Heat a frying pan, about 30 cm/ 12 inches in diameter, and brush it with a little clarified butter. Add a ladleful of batter, quickly swirl it around to cover the base of the pan, and cook the pancake for 30 seconds, then turn it over with a palette knife and cook on the other side for 30 seconds. Make more pancakes in this way until all the batter is used; there should be 12 pancakes in all.

Using a whisk, mix the pastry cream with the orange zest and juice. Spread a spoonful of this mixture over each pancake and roll them up. Arrange the filled pancakes on a baking sheet and sprinkle with icing sugar. Glaze them under a very hot salamander or grill, then place two pancakes on each plate, lifting them with a palette knife. Serve at once.

TUTTI FRUTTI CHOUX PUFFS

100 G/3½ OZ WILD OR SMALL
   STRAWBERRIES
100 G/3½ OZ BILBERRIES
100 G/3½ OZ REDCURRANTS
250 G/9 OZ CHOUX PASTE
   (½ QUANTITY, PAGE 30)
250 ML/8 FL OZ WHIPPING CREAM,
   CHILLED
40 G/1½ OZ ICING SUGAR,
   PLUS EXTRA FOR DUSTING
1 TEASPOON VANILLA ESSENCE

SERVES 4

Preheat the oven to 220°C/
425°F/Gas Mark 7. If necessary,
delicately wash and drain the fruit,
then hull or top and tail.

Using a piping bag fitted with a
plain nozzle, pipe four large choux
puffs on to a baking sheet. Dip a
fork into cold water and mark the
tops lightly with the back of the
fork, dipping it into cold water
each time. This will help the pastry
to develop evenly as it cooks. Bake
the puffs for 20 minutes, reducing
the oven temperature to 200°C/
400°F/Gas Mark 6 after 10 minutes.

When the puffs are cooked,
transfer them to a wire rack. Using
a serrated knife, cut off a 'hat' four-
fifths of the way up each puff.

In a bowl, whip the cream with
the icing sugar and vanilla essence
until it forms soft peaks. Fill a
piping bag fitted with a fluted
nozzle with this cream and pipe a
small rosette into each puff. Pile a
mixture of the fruits into the puffs,
then pipe a band of cream around
the puffs. Serve at once, or place in
the refrigerator for no more than
1 hour before serving, dusted with
icing sugar.

HOT GRAND MARNIER SOUFFLÉS
with orange segments

25 G/1 OZ BUTTER, SOFTENED

175 G/6 OZ CASTER SUGAR

3 ORANGES, PEELED AND DIVIDED
INTO SEGMENTS, ALL PITH AND
MEMBRANE REMOVED

300 G/11 OZ PASTRY CREAM
(PAGE 29)

3 TABLESPOONS GRAND MARNIER

8 EGG WHITES

4 SPRIGS OF MINT

2 TABLESPOONS ICING SUGAR

SERVES 4

Brush the insides of four small soufflé dishes, about 10 cm/ 4 inches in diameter, with the softened butter. Tip 25 g/1 oz of the caster sugar into one of the dishes and rotate it so that the interior is well coated with sugar. Tip the excess sugar into the next dish and repeat the process with all the dishes.

Preheat the oven to 190°C/ 375°F/Gas Mark 5 and put in a baking sheet to heat.

Reserve the eight best orange segments for the garnish and cut the remaining segments lengthways into three.

Put the pastry cream into a bowl, stand this in a bain-marie (see page 10) and warm gently. Whisk in the Grand Marnier.

Beat the egg whites with an electric mixer or by hand until half-risen, then add the remaining 150 g/5 oz of caster sugar and beat until the mixture forms soft peaks. Still using the whisk, fold one-third of the egg whites into the pastry cream, then very delicately fold in the rest of the whites, using a spatula.

Half-fill the soufflé dishes with the mixture, divide the cut orange segments between the dishes, then fill them up with soufflé mixture and smooth the surface with a palette knife. Using the tip of a knife, ease the mixture away from the edges of the dishes.

Stand the soufflé dishes on the heated baking sheet and cook in the oven for 7–8 minutes. As soon as they come out of the oven, arrange two of the reserved orange segments and a mint sprig on each soufflé and dust with icing sugar. Place each soufflé dish on a plate and serve immediately.

APPLE HEDGEHOG

600 ML/1 PINT APPLE JUICE
8 EGG YOLKS
70 G/2½ OZ CASTER SUGAR
6 GELATINE LEAVES, SOAKED IN COLD
   WATER, THEN WELL DRAINED
4 TABLESPOONS CALVADOS
12 TABLESPOONS APPLE PURÉE
300 ML/½ PINT WHIPPING CREAM
   AND 85 G/3 OZ ICING SUGAR,
   WHIPPED TO SOFT PEAKS

APPLE CRISPS

4 DESSERT APPLES, NOT TOO RIPE
40 G/1½ OZ CASTER SUGAR
40 G/1½ OZ ICING SUGAR

SERVES 6

Pour the apple juice into a saucepan and simmer to reduce by one-third.

In a bowl, whisk the egg yolks with the caster sugar to a light ribbon consistency. Still whisking, pour the boiling apple juice on to the mixture. Return this to the saucepan and cook over very low heat, without boiling, stirring continuously with a wooden spoon until the custard is thick enough to coat the back of the spoon. Off the heat, stir in the drained gelatine, then pass the custard through a sieve into a bowl. Set aside, stirring from time to time. When almost cold, use a whisk to fold in the Calvados, apple purée and whipped cream. Divide between six moulds, about 10 cm/4 inches in diameter, and place in the freezer for 1 hour, or in the refrigerator for 4 hours, until the mousses are set but not too firm.

Preheat the oven to 180°C/350°F/Gas Mark 4.

For the apple crisps, halve the apples horizontally and use a plain 3 cm/1¼ inch diameter pastry cutter to cut around the core to make cylinders of apple, leaving behind the core and pips. Cut the cylinders into the thinnest possible discs. Spread the discs over a greased baking sheet and sprinkle each with a pinch of caster sugar. Cook for 8 minutes, then turn them over one at a time and cook for a further 4 minutes. Transfer to a wire rack.

Briefly dip the base of each mould into very hot water. With your fingertips, lightly push one side of the mousse and invert the mould on to a serving plate. Poke the apple crisps into the mousses to resemble hedgehog spines and dust with a little icing sugar. Serve at once.

THE BASICS

QUICK PUFF PASTRY

This pastry will rise about 30% less than classic puff pastry, but it is much easier to prepare.

500 G/1 LB 2 OZ FLOUR, PLUS
    EXTRA FOR TURNING
500 G/1 LB 2 OZ FIRM BUTTER,
    CUT INTO CUBES (TAKE OUT OF
    THE REFRIGERATOR 1 HOUR
    BEFORE USING)
1 TEASPOON SALT
250 ML/8 FL OZ ICED WATER

MAKES 1.2 KG/2¾ LB
Put the flour on to the work surface or into a bowl, and make a well in the centre. Add the butter and salt to the well. Work the ingredients together using the fingertips of your right hand, gradually drawing in the flour with your left hand.

When the mixture resembles breadcrumbs, pour in the iced water and gradually work it into the pastry, without kneading. When the pastry comes together to form a dough, but still contains small flakes of butter, roll it out on a lightly floured surface, rolling away from you, to form a 40 x 20 cm/ 16 x 8 inch rectangle.

Fold in the ends, as if folding a letter, to make three equal layers. Turn the pastry through 90 degrees and repeat the rolling process. These are the first two turns. Wrap the pastry in clingfilm and chill in the refrigerator for 30 minutes.

After 30 minutes, take it out of the refrigerator and roll out again, making two more turns. The pastry is now ready. Roll to the required shape, place on a dampened baking sheet and refrigerate for 20 minutes before use.

Alternatively the pastry can be wrapped in clingfilm and stored in the refrigerator.

PASTRY CREAM

6 EGG YOLKS
125 G/4 OZ CASTER SUGAR
40 G/1½ OZ FLOUR
500 ML/16 FL OZ MILK
1 VANILLA POD, SPLIT
A LITTLE BUTTER OR ICING SUGAR

For coffee or chocolate pastry cream, omit the vanilla pod and use a little instant coffee or cocoa powder, to taste. If using cocoa powder, use a little less flour and a little extra sugar.

MAKES ABOUT 750 G/ 1 LB 10 OZ

In a large bowl, whisk the egg yolks with about one-third of the caster sugar until pale and thick (a light ribbon consistency). Sift the flour over the mixture and mix in thoroughly.

Bring the milk to the boil with the remaining sugar and the vanilla pod. As soon as it begins to bubble, pour one-third into the egg mixture, stirring all the time. Pour back into the saucepan and bring to the boil over a very low heat, stirring all the time. Allow to bubble for 2 minutes, then pour the pastry cream into a bowl. To prevent a skin from forming, dot with a few flakes of butter or dust lightly with icing sugar.

Pastry cream can be stored in the refrigerator for 36 hours.

CHOUX PASTE

125 ML/4 FL OZ WATER
125 ML/4 FL OZ MILK
100 G/3½ OZ BUTTER, FINELY
    DICED
½ TEASPOON FINE SALT
¾ TEASPOON SUGAR
150 G/5 OZ FLOUR, SIFTED
4 EGGS
EGGWASH (1 EGG YOLK MIXED WITH
    2 TEASPOONS MILK AND A PINCH
    OF SALT) − OPTIONAL

MAKES 22–25 SMALL CHOUX PUFFS OR ÉCLAIRS

Put the water, milk, butter, salt and sugar into a saucepan and boil over a high heat for 1 minute. Make sure that the mixture is well combined and then remove from the heat. Add the flour at once, stirring with a wooden spoon to make a smooth paste.

Return the pan to the heat and stir for 1 minute. Be careful not to let the paste dry too much or it will crack during cooking. Transfer the paste to a bowl and beat in the eggs one at a time. Beat the paste until very smooth.

If the pastry is not to be used immediately, spread a little eggwash over the surface to prevent a crust from forming.

Choux paste can be stored in an airtight container in the refrigerator for 3 days or in the freezer for up to 1 week.

THE MASTER CHEFS

SOUPS
ARABELLA BOXER

MEZE, TAPAS AND ANTIPASTI
AGLAIA KREMEZI

PASTA SAUCES
GORDON RAMSAY

RISOTTO
MICHELE SCICOLONE

SALADS
CLARE CONNERY

MEDITERRANEAN
ANTONY WORRALL THOMPSON

VEGETABLES
PAUL GAYLER

LUNCHES
ALASTAIR LITTLE

COOKING FOR TWO
RICHARD OLNEY

FISH
RICK STEIN

CHICKEN
BRUNO LOUBET

SUPPERS
VALENTINA HARRIS

THE MAIN COURSE
ROGER VERGÉ

ROASTS
JANEEN SARLIN

WILD FOOD
ROWLEY LEIGH

PACIFIC
JILL DUPLEIX

CURRIES
PAT CHAPMAN

HOT AND SPICY
PAUL AND JEANNE RANKIN

THAI
JACKI PASSMORE

CHINESE
YAN-KIT SO

VEGETARIAN
KAREN LEE

DESSERTS
MICHEL ROUX

CAKES
CAROLE WALTER

COOKIES
ELINOR KLIVANS

THE MASTER CHEFS

Text © copyright 1996 Michel Roux

Michel Roux has asserted his right to be
identified as the Author of this Work.

Photographs © copyright 1996 Simon Wheeler

First published in 1996 by
WEIDENFELD & NICOLSON
THE ORION PUBLISHING GROUP
ORION HOUSE
5 UPPER ST MARTIN'S LANE
LONDON WC2H 9EA

British Library Cataloguing-in-Publication data
A catalogue record for this book is available
from the British Library.

ISBN 0 297 83648 X

DESIGNED BY THE SENATE
EDITOR MAGGIE RAMSAY
FOOD STYLIST JOY DAVIES
ASSISTANT KATY HOLDER